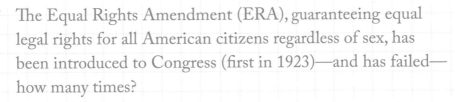
1 The Equal Rights Amendment (ERA), guaranteeing equal legal rights for all American citizens regardless of sex, has been introduced to Congress (first in 1923)—and has failed—how many times?

   a. Fewer than 10

   b. 143

   c. 425

   d. More than 1,100

2 Out of 195 countries, how many countries specifically guarantee equality between women and men in their constitutions (as of 2014)?

   a. Fewer than 10

   b. 143

   c. All of them

   d. 100

3 There are 132 million young girls around the world who are not in school, not receiving an education. Why?

   a. They are needed at home to help with life-sustaining chores like fetching water miles away.

   b. They lack access to feminine hygiene products that enable them to leave their homes.

   c. Parents cannot afford much tuition and since boys are favored in the family, the boys go to school.

   d. All of the above.

4

The U.S. women's suffrage movement fought long and hard for a woman's right to vote. In what year did the 19th Amendment, granting this right, become law?

    a. 1890

    b. 1900

    c. 1920

    d. 1939

5

Black women were still mostly unable to vote even after the 19th Amendment became law. Why?

    a. They were made to pay an expensive "poll tax."

    b. They were forced to undergo rigged tests (reading, reciting, interpreting the Constitution).

    c. They were sometimes beaten, sometimes jailed, when trying to vote.

    d. All of the above.

Girls Solve EVERYTHING

Stories of
WOMEN
ENTREPRENEURS
Building a
Better World

Catherine Thimmesh

ILLUSTRATED BY Melissa Sweet

HOUGHTON MIFFLIN HARCOURT
Boston   New York

Copia™ is a trademark of Go Copia, PBC.
Embrace® is a registered trademark of Embrace Innovations.
Dress for Success® is a registered trademark of Dress for Success Worldwide Corporation.
Good on You® is a registered trademark of Good On You Pty Ltd PROPRIETARY COMPANY
AUSTRALIA.

The illustrations are mixed media.
The text was set in Adobe Caslon Pro.

The Library of Congress Cataloging-in-Publication Data is on file.
ISBN: 978-0-358-10634-0

Manufactured in Italy
ROTO 10 9 8 7 6 5 4 3 2 1
4500836122

To Vicki and Steve Palmquist—for their many years of friendship, and for the many ways their work enriches the children's literature community

—C.T.

To Amelia and the next generation of makers, designers, and innovators

—M.S.

SOLUTION STORIES

INTRODUCTION

An app. A grilled cheese sandwich. A circus.

Each one, an innovative solution to a complex social problem—be it the ethical and sustainable practices of fashion, a second chance for people with a criminal record, or even the awareness and elimination of domestic abuse. Each one, a business product or business model developed by a woman to impact and improve people's lives.

Consider the app Good on You, created by Sandra Capponi (along with a cofounder) in 2015 in Australia. Operating via grant money and crowdfunding, the app allows consumers to literally "wear their values" and make purchasing decisions that give them influence over large corporations.

The Good On You app rates more than two thousand clothing brands on their sustainability practices, their efforts to reduce pollution and carbon emissions, and their fair (or unfair or abusive) practices toward workers and animals. A poor rating can translate into substantially fewer sales for the brand—lowering profits for the corporation—and thus be a huge incentive for them to change their practices for the better.

SOJOURNER TRUTH

People who use a business to confront enormous social problems (whether the business is for-profit, nonprofit, or a hybrid between the two) are known as "social entrepreneurs" or "social innovators."

And, as it turns out, some of the most creative and innovative entrepreneurs are women.

Historically, women have always helped mend the social fabric. From a group of ladies in 1812 who formed the Boston Fragment Society to help the poor, to Sojourner Truth who worked to abolish slavery, to Elizabeth Cady Stanton who advocated for women's rights . . . women have actively and aggressively volunteered to improve our communities and the world at large.

And the world has improved in significant ways! Though at times it feels as if our world is beset by constant, insurmountable problems, the facts point to a world that has made enormous progress and continues to do so.

Two hundred years ago, to take just one example, 85% of the world's population lived in extreme poverty; thirty years ago, that number was 37%; by 2018, just 10% of the population lived in extreme poverty.

Progress happens because people *solve* problems. And social entrepreneurs are problem-solvers at their core.

Social entrepreneurs differ from volunteers in that they are trying to create long-term *business* solutions (as opposed to charitable or activist solutions) to these overwhelming problems.

And while the terms "social entrepreneur" and "social innovator" are relatively new, the actual practice of women innovating through business for the social good stretches back more than two hundred years (and probably further).

One early innovator was Catherine (Katy) Ferguson, who created the first Sabbath School in 1793 in New York City to teach poor children and orphans how to read. Katy was a freed slave and was, herself, illiterate. But she felt deeply that children needed love, discipline, and the ability to read in order to grow up to be productive

CATHERINE FERGUSON

citizens in the community—and she was determined to provide those things.

Because these poor children were forced laborers (working ten-hour days, six days a week), Katy opened her school on Sundays—first in her home, later in other locations. To tutor the kids, she brought in instructors who taught a combination of secular and religious lessons. Since no one paid tuition, Katy solicited donations and sold her specialty wedding cakes to get the money necessary to buy books and pay the instructors. Katy's Sabbath School was replicated across the city and eventually the nation (though in later years, the lessons were mostly religious in nature).

Social entrepreneurs are disrupters. They see problems, and rather than accept the status quo or the oft-heard phrase "this is how it's always been done," they bulldoze the old system and create a new one.

FLORENCE NIGHTINGALE

Florence Nightingale, for example, traveled from England in 1855 to volunteer at the Crimean War front with the intent of nursing wounded soldiers. Arriving to find thousands of sick and dying men in filthy clothes, in overcrowded surroundings, with rats and fleas in abundance and basic medical supplies nonexistent, she instead rebuilt an entirely collapsed hospital system—with no mandate, no oversight, and no monetary compensation.

She cleaned and sterilized everything, introduced the necessity of clean towels and soap, completely reorganized the hospital, devised a method for meticulous record keeping, and introduced nightly visits to give mental and emotional comfort to the patients. Her changes were responsible for a rapid and dramatic decline in patient deaths—down from 50% to 2%. Completely revolutionizing how hospitals operate, Florence Nightingale is credited as the founder of modern-day nursing.

Creative thinking and innovative approaches to solving problems are truly what set social entrepreneurs apart.

EMILY HUNT TURNER

Open a grilled cheese sandwich restaurant to tackle a pressing civil justice issue? Why not? At least that's what Emily Hunt Turner thought when she decided to create her Minneapolis-based nonprofit, All Square, in 2018.

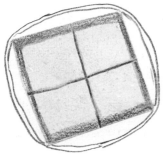

Both a restaurant and educational institute, it was created to give formerly imprisoned individuals a second chance—a second chance to work, gain new skills, get their lives back on track, and reintegrate into society.

Employment for former convicts is an enormous problem in America. When men and women are released from jail, having paid their debt to society (meaning they should now be "all square" in the eyes of the law and society), they are consistently discriminated against when searching for employment and housing and when obtaining government assistance. Because of these roadblocks, people often become desperate, commit crimes, and end up back in jail.

But at All Square, former inmates are now "fellows"—with a job that pays a living wage, along with mandatory classes at the institute. The fellows not only learn things such as making a budget and applying for jobs and schools but also take in-depth classes in entrepreneurship and law. Signs indicate that Emily and her team have cooked up a recipe for success. In fact, *Time* magazine named All Square one of "The World's 100 Greatest Places of 2019." It's a recipe that has

Since 1997, Isatou Ceesay and her organization, Women Initiative - The Gambia, has trained more than two thousand Gambian women to reclaim plastic waste, recycle it, and craft it into wallets and purses—cleaning up and protecting the environment while simultaneously empowering women to learn business skills and earn income.

just the right ingredients—and they plan to replicate it in cities nationwide.

While many people see the world's sprawling problems as "too complicated for me to do anything about," social entrepreneurs see the same problems and think, *Someone has to do something—it might as well be me.* They dismiss common phrases such as "it's impossible" and "it can't be done" because they intuitively believe that a solution exists somewhere, and it's better to try and fail than never to have tried at all.

On the face of it, using a circus show to end the centuries-old, culturally accepted practice of domestic abuse in Mongolia does sound rather impossible. Until one learns that Chimgee Haltarhuu and her company, Mission Manduhai—funded through paid circus performances and donations—are doing exactly that. Chimgee, a circus performer and teacher—formerly with Ringling Brothers and herself a survivor of abuse—has traveled back to her native home of Mongolia every year since 2010 to provide free circus shows and educate the audiences on preventing domestic abuse.

CHIMGEE HALTARHUU

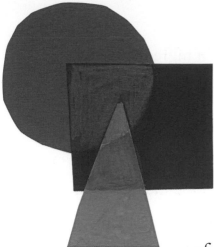

The free circus entertainment is the lure—drawing hundreds of people (mostly families with children) to Chimgee and her group of performers. She speaks briefly before each performance (and typically does around fifteen shows per visit throughout Mongolia), distributing upward of five thousand educational flyers throughout rural villages and sponsoring a hotline for abused women to call to get help.

Chimgee knows she can't change the culture in one day, or even one year—or two or three. But she can spread the message to the children—planting the seeds of change year after year where hopefully they'll take root and grow in the younger generation . . . so that when those kids reach adulthood, they can collectively choose to break the cycle.

Today, in cubicles and classrooms, coffee shops and conference rooms, and even in cornfields, women and girls are problem solving to make a difference. They are combining their empathy and desire to change the world with innovation and creativity.

They are imagining. And reimagining. They are thinking and researching and talking. "What if . . . ?" they ask. "How about . . . ?" they wonder. "Aha!" they exclaim.

And gradually their problem solving gives rise to hope . . . and to businesses that touch all our lives, that inspire and energize our own creativity to go out and change the world—women and men, girls and boys alike. These are a few of their stories.

TALIA LEMAN
Helping Kids Make a Difference

One random kid.

That's all it takes to make a difference in the world.

Because if one random kid enlists ten other kids to help, the difference they can collectively make multiplies and grows. And if that one random kid is somehow able to connect with *thousands* of other kids, the difference they can make is . . . well, pretty incredible.

And that's exactly what happened when Talia Leman—just one random ten-year-old in Iowa—decided that she wanted to help the victims of Hurricane Katrina in 2005. Their total devastation and loss played out in heart-wrenching images day after day on the news—most of New Orleans under water, people on rooftops waiting to be rescued, a million people suddenly homeless.

"A lot of time," says Talia, "I see people not taking action because issues seem so complicated and complex, and often the complexity of the issue discourages people from trying to make a difference. The benefit of kids stepping up is that they are not dissuaded by complexity. They respond to the fundamental human needs they see in times of crisis."

That was certainly true for Talia.

It began with Talia telling her mom she wanted to do something to help the hurricane victims, something big enough to have an impact.

Halloween was coming, and Talia and her mom landed on the idea to trick-or-treat for coins instead of candy—and to get as many kids as possible to join. When her mom was truly convinced Talia wanted to do this—in part based on the two-page, handwritten plan Talia had made to raise a million dollars—she said okay and then sent the plan to a local TV station, hoping for an interview. From there, trick-or-treating for coins snowballed.

"What I ended up accomplishing was really unexpected," says Talia. "But I think sometimes we just have to put ourselves out there and make room for the unexpected."

After the TV interview, the stars aligned. A local woman (Anne Ginther) with a marketing background reached out and partnered with Talia (and her mom). Thinking bigger, Talia managed to convince the local Hy-Vee grocery chain to print and distribute more than eight million trick-or-treat bags with her message on them. They partnered with the well-known and respected nonprofit UNICEF and were featured on the morning show *TODAY* with a fun hook: Talia's little brother came along, expressing opposition to her idea—making him her official Chief Operating Nemesis. He. Was. Very. Much. Against. This. Whole. Plan. (He wanted candy!)

Since its inception in 2005, Talia's nonprofit has coordinated and mobilized more than twelve million kids from more than twenty countries. They have built schools, funded water pumps, and provided funding for medical care, to name just a few projects.

On Halloween, Talia's brother did get candy. Talia—and thousands of other random kids who helped trick-or-treat for coins—got more than *ten million dollars* for Hurricane Katrina relief!

UNICEF delivered truckloads of kits—packed with school supplies, art materials, and recreational toys—to thousands of kids who had lost everything and were living in shelters.

Talia's overwhelming success at harnessing kids to trick-or-treat for hurricane relief led her to take a giant leap forward and cocreate an online social nonprofit. Called RandomKid, its mission is to empower "any random kid" to solve problems by offering free resources kids might need—from connecting them with other like-minded kids to giving them services such as consulting, product development, web pages, media, event planning, and even seed funding (a small amount of up-front cash to get things started).

RandomKid operates as a nonprofit, using a pay-it-forward funding model. Ten percent of all money raised by a project is deposited into its community fund to help pay the costs for the next random kid with a great idea.

"A lot of organizations raise money for causes [that people can simply donate to]," explains Talia. *"But I don't really think there's much out there that guides youth step by step, giving them the ability to create the change they are inspired to create."*

With RandomKid, Talia hoped to replicate the support

and encouragement she had been given when she went to others for help.

Thousands of RandomKid projects have been undertaken. Katie's Krops grew vegetable gardens and donated thousands of pounds of fresh produce to those in need. A classroom of sixth grade students in Ohio collected crutches and canes for people who had lost their limbs in a devastating earthquake in Haiti. And two siblings from Indiana collected and recycled old cell phones with AT&T, which in turn donated cell phone minutes to soldiers.

"It's really giving kids the tools to make change and become leaders," says Talia. "It allows them to learn through the process and empowers them to do whatever they want to do for the world."

Have an idea to help others?

All it takes is one random kid . . . and another and another and another . . .

JEROO BILLIMORIA
Connecting Street Kids with Help

Ten, nine, eight . . . and the countdown begins.

Countdowns usually mean there's excitement brewing—a rocket launch, perhaps, or maybe a game of hide-and-seek.

But in India, 10-9-8 means the very opposite of fun and games. Instead, the numbers are a call of distress from one of the country's millions of street children—children (generally ages six to twelve) who live alone on the streets of India, fending for themselves to stay alive and unharmed.

By dialing 1-0-9-8, a street child in India is connected to Childline India—a twenty-four-hour emergency phone service—founded by Jeroo Billimoria in 1996 to help street children in Mumbai.

"I was working with street kids in India," recalls Jeroo, *"and they used to call up my house at all hours because they needed help. And most professional social workers work from nine to five—but these kids needed help after hours—so then I would go and help them as much as I could."*

The problem, of course, was that Jeroo, on her own, could not possibly answer every call for help—could not possibly provide instant, in-person support round-the-clock. The solution, Jeroo realized, was a single point of contact for the children that would, in turn, send them the help they needed.

It took the government three years to issue the toll-free number to Jeroo and

The centralized crisis number handles any emergency that the street kids might have. A broken leg or medical illness? Check. An empty stomach in need of a meal? A safe place to shelter for the night? Check and check. Help to escape abuse, violence, drug use, or trafficking? Help for runaways or abandoned kids? To all, check. By 2018, the crisis hotline had handled more than forty million distress calls.

Childline. In the meantime, she connected and partnered with various organizations that already provided specific, specialized services—such as sheltering or medical help—that the street kids needed.

"A key part of the concept was that I wasn't trying to reinvent the wheel," explains Jeroo. "Childline built no new shelters, no new infrastructure. We used services that already existed, calling on the expertise of others in child protection."

When Jeroo finally got the toll-free number from the government, she was initially dismayed, thinking that the assigned number 1-0-9-8 would be too difficult for many of the young kids to memorize. But one of the children pointed out that it was actually easy—just count down from ten: 10-9-8—and little kids could learn it on their fingers. It was a brilliant and extremely helpful observation.

Dialing 10-9-8 on a public pay phone was free and would connect children directly to Childline. But for the crisis line to work, the street kids had to know about it. So Jeroo and her team did a lot of sitting on street corners, waiting at train stops and other spots, and going out at night to communicate with the children. They held workshops. And fun fairs. They enlisted the kids themselves to help . . . and little by little the word got out.

"There were several obstacles," says Jeroo, "but I think the main

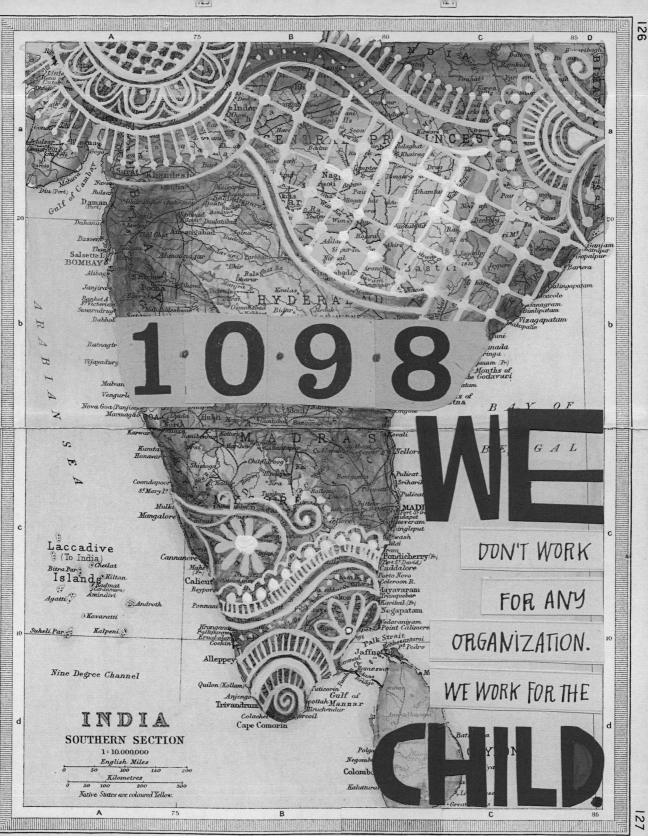

one was people not believing in the concept—that the street children would even call. There was no proof of concept anywhere in the world that it would work."

And without proof of concept, fundraising—asking people to donate money to operate the nonprofit organization—was extremely difficult. Much of the early work was done by volunteers—including some of the street kids themselves.

From the children's perspective, they initially didn't believe help would come if they called the number. So a lot of the early calls were kids just testing to see if the call resulted in a person showing up to help them. (It always did.)

When it became clear that the pilot program in Mumbai was a success—and "proof of concept" had been shown— Jeroo then worked with the government to expand Childline India throughout the country.

"If you see a problem, you can always run or turn your face and walk away," says Jeroo. "Or you

can try to resolve it whatever way you can."

Jeroo firmly believes that most problems cannot be solved by a single individual or organization—but rather, that significant change happens collaboratively.

Childline India has part-nered with more than seven hundred organizations—help-ing children in immediate crisis but also, crucially, helping them long-term: following up on the initial call with as many visits and resources as it takes, trying to get kids off the streets and back into homes.

Jeroo later founded Child Helpline International, a "collective impact organization," with member helplines in 146 different countries that share knowledge, data, and other information to help advocate for children worldwide. The Helplines field more than twenty million calls and texts every year.

1-0-9-8 . . . These are numbers, of course, not letters that form words. And yet, for the most vulnerable children in India, these numbers spell H-e-l-p. And also . . . H-o-p-e.

WENDY KOPP
Teachers for All

Extra credit: If School "A" (in the well-off neighborhood) has iPads galore, state-of-the-art technology, up-to-date textbooks, and dedicated teachers in every classroom, and School "B" (in the low-income neighborhood) is beset by shortages—not only of textbooks and technology but also, most importantly, of teachers—which students are more likely to receive the better education?

When Wendy Kopp was a senior in college studying public policy, one of the things that really bothered her were the inequities of the educational system. Too often, where you were born (or where you lived) determined the type of education you received. Equally bothersome was that even with a shortage of teachers, distinguished college graduates were recruited to "follow the money" and head to Wall Street or into other lucrative fields rather than into education.

"I had organized a conference alongside some other students at Princeton about improving our education system," explained Wendy to NPR. *"[. . .] And the [students] were saying, 'We had no idea there was a need for teachers in urban and rural areas; we would teach.'*

"And it was really sitting there," Wendy continued, *"that I thought of this idea. Why* aren't *we channeling these people's energy into teaching?"*

Her idea was to form a national teacher corps— Teach For America—that would take outstanding college grads, train them, and have them serve as teachers in urban and rural communities for two years.

During her research, Wendy talked to the head of

Teach For America was launched in 1989, and since then, sixty thousand graduates have committed two years to teach in urban and rural public schools. Today, 85% of them continue to work in education or in careers supporting low-income communities.

human resources in the Los Angeles Unified School District to see if he'd hire Teach For America recruits (talented graduates from competitive colleges and universities, but without a specific degree in education) and place them as teachers in needed schools.

"I remember that conversation," said Wendy, who also wrote *about the exchange in her book,* One Day, All Children. *"[He] just looked at the list [of colleges where we were recruiting] and started laughing. 'I'll tell you what: you get people from Stanford who want to teach in my school system, I'll hire all five hundred of them.' And that was the reaction I got everywhere."*

Before Wendy had even secured all the necessary funding, her team began recruiting. And maybe it was youthful idealism or a desire to prove that the "Me Generation" was woefully misnamed, or perhaps it was the earnestness of the flyer asking recipients if they wanted to be part of a *movement* to ensure America was living up to its promise of equal opportunity for all, beginning with education. But whatever the reason, twenty-five hundred college students wanted in on Teach For America.

"My greatest asset was my inexperience, my complete naïveté," Wendy wrote in her book. *"I was convinced both that this had to happen, and that it could happen—and it could start on a significant scale right from the start."*

KIDS DON'T FALL BEHIND BECAUSE THEY LACK POTENTIAL... THEY FALL BEHIND BECAUSE THEY JUST HAVEN'T BEEN GIVEN THE OPPORTUNITES THEY DESERVE.

Teach For America inspired others outside the United States to contact Wendy about starting similar programs in their countries. In 2007, Teach For All was launched and includes organizations in more than fifty countries.

The idea was multifaceted from the get-go. First, Wendy most certainly wanted energetic, intelligent, eager graduates to fill positions where teachers were desperately needed—such as Los Angeles, New York City, and rural North Carolina. But additionally, she wanted Teach For America to create a pipeline of people who would tackle educational inequalities, not only from the classroom but also from other leadership positions: as principals, policymakers, and advocates.

Also from the get-go, there were problems upon problems: obtaining funding (soliciting money from foundations, private donors, government organizations); securing the schools to place and pay five hundred teacher recruits (Wendy's ambitious out-of-the-starting-gate goal); and then handling the applications . . .

"We had all these applications," Wendy told NPR. *"We had underestimated, of course, everything, like what to do with two thousand five hundred applications!"*

Her small team managed to get through all the applications and interviews, settle on the first batch of recruits, have experienced teachers and educators train them (in just five weeks), and send them off to schools in desperate need of teachers—

full of energy, enthusiasm, empathy, and a sincere desire to make a difference in their students' lives.

And it's working.

In Atlanta, for example, a teacher helped students advocate for themselves—and also for the passage of the DREAM Act (which would grant them U.S. residency)—by using art.

In Mississippi, a teacher changed entire systems to make certain her Arabic-speaking students were able to learn.

"Over many years [now], we've come to understand what differentiates teachers who make the greatest impact on student achievement," explains Wendy.

Specific qualities, Wendy discovered, such as the ability to motivate others, having high expectations for kids from low-income communities, and the ability to navigate cultural differences, are crucial for a teacher's success.

"So we factor that into our recruitment, training, and support models as well."

Schools might always have a shortage of iPads and other gadgets. But hopefully, with Teach For America recruits joining talented, experienced educators, schools will no longer suffer shortages of bright, enthusiastic teachers. And together, they can work toward a system that recognizes that all students deserve an A+ education—and a promising future—regardless of the ZIP Code they live in.

TING SHIH
Medicine for the Masses

A billion is a lot.

If you counted every second of every minute of every hour of every day, week, and year, it would take more than thirty-one years of nonstop counting to reach a billion.

So when a class assignment dictated that graduate students "go and create a business that would impact a billion people," Ting Shih and her classmates had their work cut out for them.

"We were thinking it had to be something everyone had access to (in some form), and health care is just one of the areas that is so

important," Ting explains. "If you can solve—or improve—health care, you might very well save lives."

Still, in the beginning, Ting was thinking only about completing a classroom project, not launching a mobile health care business—which she did in 2011. Called ClickMedix, it is now used in more than twenty countries and has improved the lives of more than a million people thus far.

The problems with health care in developing countries are myriad. Patients living in rural areas are not able to easily reach doctors. Patients can't afford the high costs, and there are severe shortages of trained health care professionals.

"What we looked at first was, well, what do we have to work with?" says Ting. "And that's when we thought, well, people may not have much—maybe not enough food or electricity—but somehow they have access to a mobile phone."

And so Ting and her team decided to use the mobile phone as a tool to deliver health care to people in developing countries and remote areas.

To implement the idea, the team first shadowed doctors to find out what

Ting grew up watching the TV show *MacGyver*, where the lead character always solved problems with whatever materials were at hand. That resourcefulness always stayed with her and informed her strategies for this project.

information was needed from patients to make a diagnosis. Step two was to design a mobile app that a low-level health care worker in a rural area could easily operate—following the prompts on the app, mimicking questions doctors would ask, and then entering that data.

In sub-Saharan Africa, for example, ClickMedix helps solve dermatology issues. A health care worker can photograph a patient's skin lesions or rash; question the patient about other symptoms, such as bleeding, fever, or chills; and then send the data and images electronically to a specialist (often overseas), who renders a diagnosis and treatment plan—or, in some cases, advises the patient to get to the nearest clinic. The system also manages HIV, tuberculosis, diabetes, and other diseases.

With her graduate degree in systems engineering, Ting understood automation—and that automation worked so long as there was a specific, known process.

"I looked at things," she says, "and thought, Is this a process? And it turned out that health care is. You collect data. From the data you make a decision. Based on the decision, you do something about it— and then see if the patient gets better.

"And by automating," Ting continued, "we saw that 80% of patients can be diagnosed remotely. And so in some places, where

they wait for years to see a doctor, with this process it's less than three days [for a doctor to respond with a treatment plan]."

Ting and her team had innumerable challenges trying to create the app, the platform, and the business. And she had her share of failures along the way. The worst was that, initially, they worked with a vendor (an outside business partner) who wasn't trustworthy—and that relationship literally destroyed the first iteration of the company.

Ting says: "You're going to fail many, many times. And I think the biggest lesson is how fast you can get back up and get back at it."

But Ting believed in the concept so strongly and wanted to bring one-click medicine to the masses, so she started over on her own. Initially, she self-funded the start-up costs, then brought on investors and also used grant money to fund the business.

"If you're trying to do something new," Ting explains, *"[. . .] the naysayers, the haters, will say: 'Oh, I've seen a hundred things like that. How are you different?' But I think you know you're different. You know your solution is going to work [. . .] and you just have to get back up and keep going."*

And get up she did.

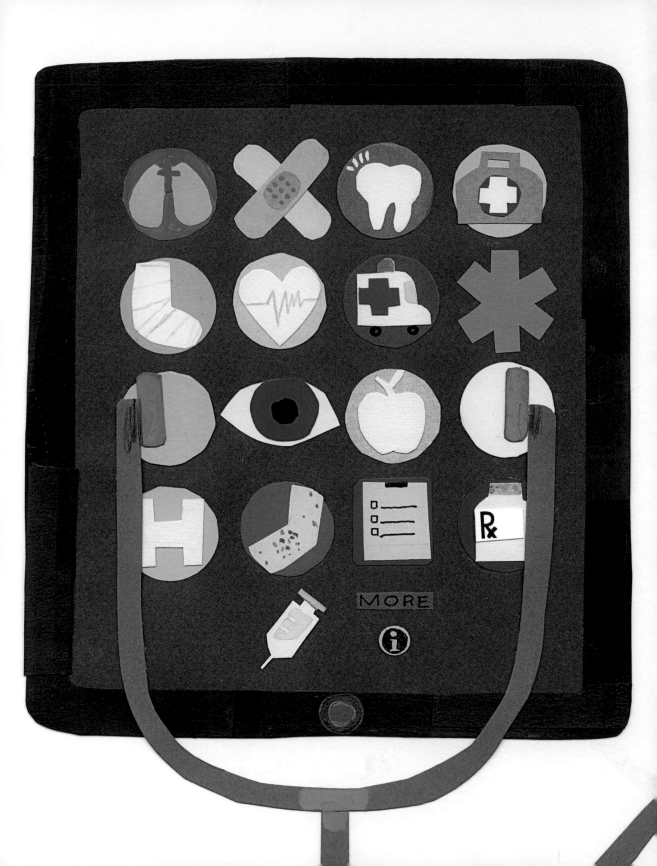

In some villages, Ting and ClickMedix are facilitating health care for more than ten times the number of patients usually seen in those areas. Connecting with a doctor via app within seventy-two hours instead of several weeks, months, or often years—while educating and empowering local nurses to improve their diagnoses and treatments—has not only saved lives but also saved countless patients from a great deal of suffering.

A billion is a lot. And if ClickMedix can successfully scale up to reach a billion people, it will truly be a global health game changer. But in the meantime, helping a million people (and still counting) is a big step in the right direction.

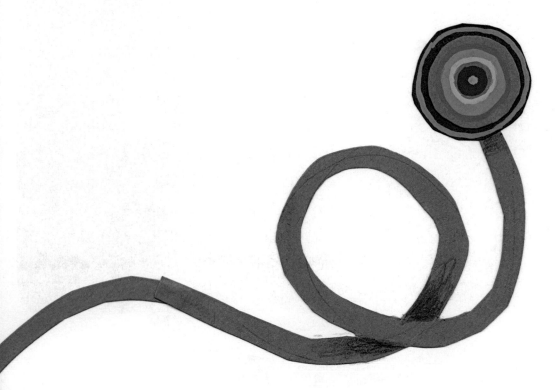

JANE CHEN
Saving Premature Newborns

After nine months in a mother's womb, a baby is born. But sometimes, babies come too soon—prematurely—weeks or even months before they are fully developed. They enter the world—teeny-tiny, fragile, and freezing cold.

In developing countries, more than a *million* premature babies die every year due to hypothermia (a dangerously low body temperature). These deaths are sadder still, knowing that an incubator could have saved them.

"We developed the Embrace Infant Warmer and founded the company Embrace Innovations," says Jane Chen. "This came out of

a class project. We didn't know what would come of it. And today, we've saved over three hundred thousand babies in over twenty countries."

Jane was a student at Stanford University in 2008 when a class assignment in Design Thinking tasked students with creating a low-cost temperature-regulating incubator—totaling just 1% of the cost of a traditional incubator, which is often prohibitively expensive in developing countries such as India, Nepal, and Somalia.

The initial research and brainstorming sessions led Jane and her three classmates (and cofounders) to conclude that more in-depth research was required to fully understand the complexities of the problem they were attempting to solve. So, cofounder Linus went on a fact-finding mission to Nepal.

In Nepal, Linus discovered that the hospitals actually had incubators—but they sat unused because there wasn't always electricity to power them. He also noted the lengthy distances between villages and hospitals, which meant premature babies delivered at home

To enhance their creative process, Jane and her teammates made a point of holding their brainstorming sessions in unique locales. Their first meeting was up in a tree, each team member sitting on a different limb, discussing how best to take the project forward.

had no immediate access to an incubator, a critical element for survival.

"So that really shifted the problem for us," Jane says. *"We realized we needed a solution that would not only sit in big-city hospitals but that could also be in very remote areas where a mother or midwife could operate the technology—and that technology could not be completely reliant on electricity."*

Their solution? A swaddling sleeping bag for infants with a built-in warming pouch that would use a phase-changing material (PCM) rather than electricity. (A PCM is a substance that releases or absorbs energy—and therefore heats or cools—as it changes in physical state from solid to liquid or vice versa. A PCM maintains a constant temperature until the phase change is complete.)

"I think the fact that I wasn't an engineer," Jane points out, *"and my engineers didn't have medical backgrounds allowed us to look at the problem in a whole new way."*

They began prototyping—making early models of a baby warmer—continuously researching, testing, and refining along the way. The beauty of prototyping is that the process is rough—using cheap materials at hand and usually a lot of duct tape!—just to get a better sense of how (or if) the idea will actually work. Jane's team went through hundreds of iterations.

"If there's a lesson here," says Jane, *"it's to keep building and*

STEP BY STEP FOR THE EMBRACE WARMER

1.

Heat the PCM pouch in hot water for twenty minutes.

2.

Insert heated pouch into special slot in the Embrace Warmer.

3.

Place baby gently inside the warmer.

Keeps temp constant at 98.6° for over 4 hours.

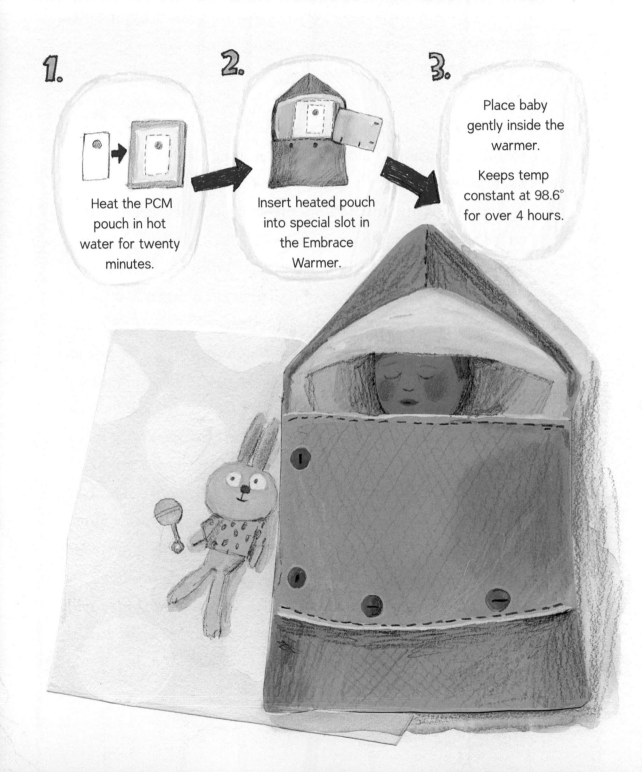

iterating and testing. A big part of the design thinking process is embracing failure. And not really looking at it as failure but as an opportunity to learn and keep improving on whatever you're doing."

One of the biggest surprises and challenges they faced with their design would have been missed altogether had the team not gone to India for another research trip.

Speaking with mothers in the villages, they heard comments such as the following:

"We don't trust Western medicine; we think it's too strong."

"If you tell me to keep the product at 98.6 degrees, I might keep it a little less, because that's too warm."

The company was launched in 2008 and now boasts three distinct products that help save the lives of preemies. Embrace Innovations is a for-profit company, selling their affordable warmers to medical supply companies, hospitals, and relief organizations. They also work with nonprofit organizations that donate warmers around the world.

"That was a really important insight," Jane explains. "Because it made us realize we needed to make the temperature indicator binary—OK/Not OK—as opposed to the numeric scale we had, so parents would know when it was in the OK range and when it needed to be heated."

Now, in many developing countries, when a **OK / Not OK** premature baby is born into the world—teeny-tiny, fragile, freezing cold, and many hours away from the nearest hospital—she is swaddled instantly into an Embrace Infant Warmer.

The odds are good that she will not only survive the night but also survive and thrive into childhood . . . and beyond.

NADIA HAMILTON
Empowering People with Special Needs

h, the old morning routine: Get yourself up. Get dressed. Gobble down breakfast. Brush your teeth. Get out the door.

But for those with autism, tackling day-to-day tasks can be overwhelming and distressing and frequently requires help from a caregiver, often keeping these individuals from attempting tasks on their own. This anxiety and dependence on others is a problem for millions of people with autism worldwide—a problem that means social inclusion and true independence are often out of reach.

Until now.

Enter Nadia Hamilton, whose younger brother with autism inspired her to solve the problem of personal autonomy by building a business that helps people with special needs integrate into society—and helps them do so with a certain degree of independence.

Nadia's innovation was an app called MagnusCards, which provides virtual decks of cards with step-by-step instructions for numerous daily tasks, such as teeth brushing, taking public transportation, and ordering food when dining out.

"I'm an artist," explains Nadia, "and when I was growing up, I utilized this talent to draw out step-by-step instructions for life skills around the home—or even if we were going out—to prepare my brother for new situations. And I'd post them on the walls of our apartment."

After she graduated from college in her native country of Canada, Nadia heard about a social business competition online. She didn't have a formal business plan, nor any business experience— just a passion to help her brother and the millions of people like him. So, on a

Nadia and her family saw that these drawings gave her brother a sense of structure and relieved his stress and fear of not being able to complete a task on his own.

whim, she entered her hand-drawn "skills cards" as an idea for a business.

And she won.

"I was given a mentor after winning the competition," explains Nadia, "and she taught me a lot in terms of business development, helping me get the product off the ground, helping me get the first customers . . . and subsequently she became the first investor in the company as well."

After winning, Nadia also researched—a lot. She talked with organizations, members of the autism community, and caregivers. One theme consistently emerged: ditch the cumbersome physical cards and go digital.

It was quite a pivot from her original thought, but she embraced the suggestion and forged ahead—raising seed money via online crowdfunding and outsourcing the initial mobile app development to China.

But still, she had no business plan to speak of. She hadn't yet figured out the funding model—or how the business would become self-sufficient and profitable. She didn't know how it would scale up to reach more people and truly have a lasting social impact.

"One day, I was on a TV show, talking about the app," Nadia explains, "and it just so happened that the Centre for Addiction and Mental Health and York University in Canada were watching.

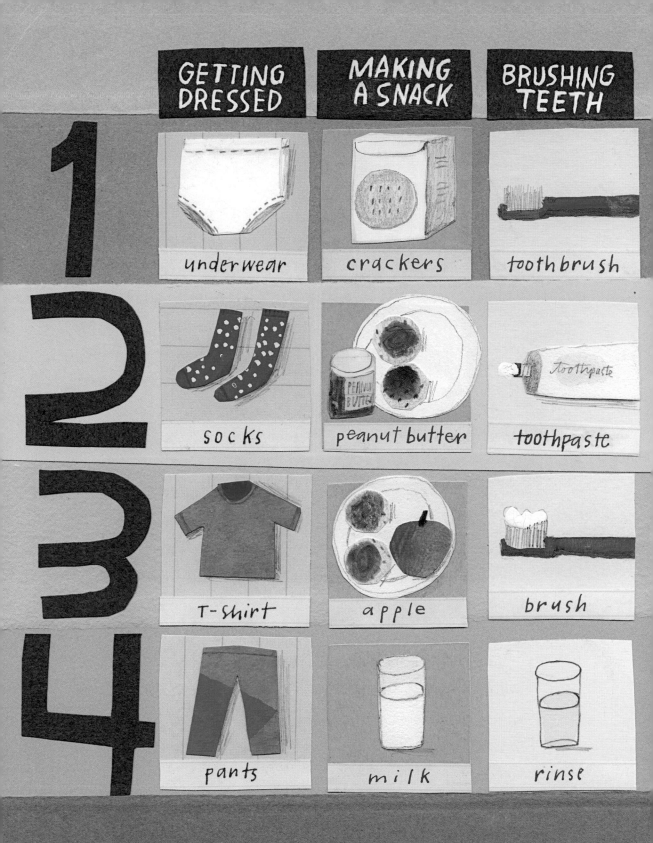

One of the many challenges Nadia faced was creating a business centered on technology even though she herself didn't have a tech background. Of course she could (and did) hire skilled workers, but it was also imperative she learn a lot of the basic tech terms and functions so she could accurately communicate her goals.

They called me and said, 'Hey, this is fantastic. Can we use this platform to create card decks for our needs?' And that's how I developed the idea of the business model!"

So her company, Magnusmode, works in tandem with corporations and organizations (and their experts) to create custom-branded skills cards.

Launched in 2017, Nadia's company already boasts more than thirty major corporate clients, including Colgate, CIBC, the Toronto Zoo, and A&W Restaurants—all of which pay to use her platform to help those with special needs navigate dental hygiene, banking, getting around at the zoo, or ordering from a menu . . . step by step by helpful step.

"This is a new way to live in the world," says Nadia. "We're shifting the perception of people with cognitive special needs as people who need to be taken care of to people who are empowered to care for themselves."

Ah, the old morning routine: Get yourself up. Swipe through an app and get yourself dressed. Swipe through again and brush your teeth. No anxiety. No fear. And no dependence on others.

By adding one ingenious app to their phone and into their routine, millions of people with special needs can now redefine their own world, step by step by step.

NANCY LUBLIN AND LISA DOROMAL

Dressed for Success

Today's the day—the big job interview.

Remember: *You never get a second chance to make a first impression.*

And don't forget: *Put your best foot forward.*

But what happens when your "best foot forward" is a sneaker with holes in it? When your closet—and your bank account—can't accommodate the dress code required for job interviews?

Luckily, there's Dress for Success—a nonprofit organization

that provides interview clothing to women in need. Founded by Nancy Lublin in 1995, it has grown to encompass more than 150 affiliates in thirty countries.

"I'd been to interviews; I knew what a nightmare getting dressed for an interview was," Nancy explained in an article for the New York Times. *"And when you think about what it is for a woman coming from a homeless shelter, or prison, or coming to this country, that must be really terrible."*

Nancy's concept for Dress for Success was a simple-enough solution: Women in need could come to the store (first housed in Nancy's apartment, then in a church basement) and be fitted for a business suit (donated by individuals and companies) and leave for their interview with everything needed to make a good first impression (suit, shoes, blouse, professional bag). All for free and all for keeps.

But, right from the beginning, there was a problem.

"I didn't know where to start!" says Nancy with a laugh.

So she talked to her law school professor, who happened to have the perfect connection. He knew of a group of nuns in Harlem doing work with struggling and disadvantaged women.

"They understood immediately the problem," Nancy explained in an interview with NPR. *"And each one had a different story of someone they were sending to a job interview who didn't show up at the interview because she felt she was inappropriately dressed.*

I LIKE BUILDING THINGS and LIKE SEEING THEM Flourish

Or showed up in a tracksuit because that was the most expensive and nicest thing she owned."

In addition, Nancy and her team set up a program to help with writing resumés and practicing interview skills. As Dress for Success quickly grew—thanks to major media exposure, such as airtime on *60 Minutes* and *Oprah*—they also started providing a full week's worth of clothing once a job was landed.

Nancy structured the nonprofit to grow via affiliate stores in other cities. The stores would uphold the central mission of the brand, but affiliate owners could innovate and run their boutiques their own way. As a nonprofit, all affiliates depend on donations of clothes and fundraising for money to keep the doors open and the lights on.

One such affiliate owner is Lisa Doromal, who opened Dress for Success in Phoenix, Arizona.

"When the client comes to Dress for Success," explains Lisa, "we set her up with

Dress for Success partnered with about two hundred organizations that referred women to them. That way, they reached more women in need (because those women were already seeking help in other areas), and just as importantly, it meant Dress for Success staff and volunteers never had to judge if a woman qualified for the free attire, because any woman was referred from these partner agencies.

a lovely personal shopper and we help her get prepared for that job interview—from the outside and the inside. We're so much more than giving women clothing (though that's where we begin). We have five programs that are really, really helping women break the cycle of poverty through job readiness and job retention."

But, as in any business, Lisa also ran into problems. She noticed her boutique had a very high rate of no-shows— women who made appointments but then didn't keep them. That happened even when Lisa called with reminders.

It turned out that many of the women had transportation barriers (and Phoenix is hard to get around without reliable transportation). Also, child-care could be very difficult to find. So, not only was the problem to dress women professionally for interviews, now the problem had multiplied to include transportation and child-care.

Dress for Success Phoenix has helped more than ten thousand women in ten years.
Internationally, the Dress for Success affiliates have served more than one million women.

Taking a page from another affiliate, Lisa invested in a customized RV trailer—bringing Dress for Success directly into individual neighborhoods—and then, she innovated.

"What we decided to do," says *Lisa, "was build a custom mobile unit*

career center that was designed to have two fitting rooms, racks of clothing, and a mini career center, so that we could bring our services out into our community."

One community member, Alwonza, was transitioning back into society after being homeless for more than a year. She described her experience with Dress for Success as making her "feel confident" in her "social skills and first impressions."

And today, after a visit to Dress for Success, more and more women are leaving the shops or mobile boutiques dressed from head to toe with self-confidence and a determination to land on their feet—this time wearing shoes without holes.

ELIZABETH STOTT
Enabling Women to Help Themselves

Silently. Stealthily. Secretly.

Under cover of darkness, they came. Women—often hidden beneath veils—slipped round to the back entrance of a boutique in Philadelphia, stashed a package by the door, and disappeared quickly into the night.

It sounds like a scene in a spy novel. But in fact, it's a scene from real life—played on repeat—upon the opening of the Philadelphia Ladies' Depository in 1832. The socially ground-breaking Ladies' Depository—founded by Elizabeth Stott (with assistance from several of her wealthy friends)—set about helping "genteel" women who'd fallen on hard financial times by selling their handcrafted goods.

But more specifically, Elizabeth didn't want to just *help* the women. She wanted a system to help these women *help themselves*.

In their first Annual Report, Elizabeth and her cofounders wrote that their goal was "to sustain in [consignors] a spirit of independence which proves a stimulant to further effort."

Elizabeth had the idea when witnessing a young mother with several children in a boutique trying, unsuccessfully, to sell some embroidery pieces to the shopkeeper for a fair price. Elizabeth followed the woman out of the shop and inquired about her circumstances. She learned the mother had recently lost her husband and desperately needed money to support her children.

Soon after that encounter, Elizabeth convened a meeting with sixteen of her female friends.

Her idea was to open a depository similar to one she

In 1832, most women did not have jobs outside the home. Those that did work, out of necessity, toiled for low wages in poor conditions. To make matters worse, society norms of the time deemed working women to be "unladylike" (paid work was considered "indelicate"), and society generally considered women who worked shameful.

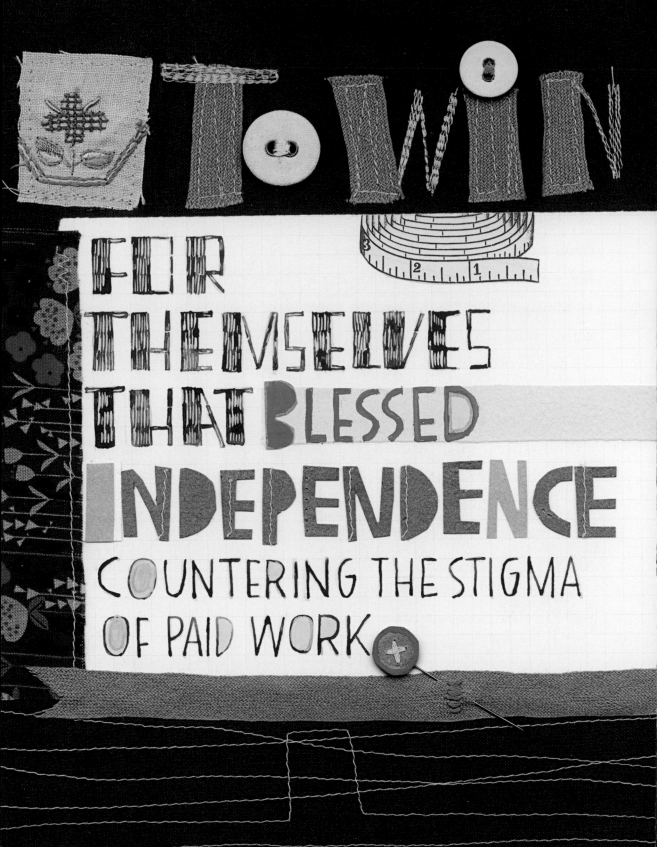

TO WIN

FOR THEMSELVES THAT BLESSED INDEPENDENCE

COUNTERING THE STIGMA OF PAID WORK

had seen while traveling in Scotland—a consignment boutique, where the genteel (i.e., high-status) women who'd fallen on hard times would have a means to earn money respectably. (She did not consider including women of all statuses at that time.)

The Philadelphia Ladies' Depository would accept work on consignment—and when that work sold, the money went directly to the woman who had created it, minus a small 6% commission fee toward the operating costs of the shop.

The model for the Philadelphia Ladies' Depository spread rapidly, and in just a few years, there were more than one hundred such consignment shops in cities across the United States. They became known as Woman's Exchanges, and they lasted more than 150 years—with a few Exchanges still in business today! (Thankfully, class, status, and perceived shame have long since been abandoned.)

And all of this would be done anonymously. The women selling their handiwork (the consignors) would drop their packages at night. In the morning, the shop manager would take in the packages and tag and display the items for sale. The clientele buying the items never knew the identity of the creator, thereby shielding those women from the shame of doing paid work.

As Elizabeth and the cofounders described in their first Annual Report, "Concealment is but a part of the object of the Ladies' Depository. Its principal design is to screen the unfortunate from the unkind treatment which they too often experience in their [interactions] with the world. Instances [. . .] which not only wounded the feelings, but tended to discourage further effort."

The Philadelphia Ladies' Depository found success rather quickly, but it also quickly found its share of challenges. So, Elizabeth and her cofounders created an advisory board to help them navigate the problems and find solutions.

First up: location. This turned out to be an easy fix—if a bit expensive. Elizabeth moved the boutique to the fashionable part of town, right smack in the middle of where their customers already were. The next concern: product control. It proved easy enough for the women to provide a sampler of their work that customers could examine and then order custom-made items if they found the sampler work satisfactory.

The Ladies' Depository proved to be a win-win for everyone—but especially for the struggling women.

"The cheerful countenances and grateful acknowledgments of many who have been relieved from difficulties, by this institution,

have cheered the Managers in their work," wrote the founders in the Annual Report.

Silently. Stealthily. Secretly. These were the first actions directed by Elizabeth Stott and undertaken by a few hundred women—not as spies, but as bona fide superheroes, working to help improve their own situations and (unbeknownst to them) paving the way for thousands and thousands like them who would join the Woman's Exchanges in the not-too-distant future.

JANE ADDAMS
Tackling Poverty

The question is straightforward: How to get out? Out of a house in the slums . . . out of a back-breaking job that pays a pittance . . . out of living a life in poverty? Out of constantly going without—without "things," for sure (new clothes, furniture, food); but also going without opportunities—in education and culture and entertainment. And looking—always looking—for that elusive path that might lead out of poverty. Who would've dreamed that the way out could come via a woman who wanted *in?*

Well, Jane Addams, for one, had such a dream.

In 1889, Jane bought a large house, along with her friend Ellen Gates Starr, in the middle of one of the poorest, working-class, immigrant neighborhoods in Chicago. They named it Hull-House, and their original plan for this "settlement house" served a dual purpose: first, to bridge the class divide by bringing culture and education directly to the poor; and second, to provide an alternative opportunity for university-educated women who didn't wish to assume a traditional domestic lifestyle. (Jane first saw a settlement house in London, run by university men.)

"The Settlement," wrote Jane Addams in her book, Twenty Years at Hull-House, *"is an experimental effort to aid in the solution of the social and industrial problems which are [brought about] by the modern conditions of life in a great city."*

The university-educated women would come and join the settlement, pay rent to reside in the house, and volunteer their time and talents working with less-fortunate people in the neighborhood—hosting lectures and readings and musical gatherings. But very soon, in addition to those educational and cultural offerings, the immediate, everyday needs of the neighbors took much of their focus.

"From the first," wrote Jane, "it seemed understood that we were ready to perform the humblest neighborhood services. We were asked

to wash the new-born babies, and to prepare the dead for burial, to nurse the sick and to 'mind the children.'"

After talking with her new neighbors, it became clear to Jane that the women desperately needed a place to bring their children. And so, the first major initiative of Hull-House was opening a kindergarten. Within three weeks, seventy kids were on a waiting list. A day nursery soon followed.

Providing daycare and kindergarten gave women with children the support they needed to go to work or school—two crucial elements for people trying to improve their lives and escape poverty.

But Hull-House didn't stop there. Next came a club for teenage boys, then cooking and sewing classes for the girls. A public gymnasium, a public playground, and a public pool (all Chicago firsts) would soon follow. Hull-House even offered immigrants citizenship preparation classes (the very first in the nation)!

Of course, all of these efforts were costly—which presented seemingly never-ending challenges for Jane.

"We were often bitterly pressed for money and worried by the prospect of unpaid bills," wrote Jane. "We gave up one golden scheme after another because we could not afford it; we cooked the meals and kept the books and washed the windows [. . .]. But [. . .] I

always believed that money would be given when we had once clearly reduced the Settlement idea to the actual deed."

Perhaps most significantly, Jane and the Hull-House residents listened and learned from their neighbors—most of them immigrants, most poverty-stricken. The Hull-House women became advocates for

Jane opened Hull-House with a small amount of money she had inherited. But to keep it running, the business model included collecting rent from the university women residents, along with quite a bit of fundraising and some government grants. Hull-House—which grew to a compound of thirteen buildings— would keep its doors open for more than a hundred years.

their neighbors—first investigating problems and gathering facts and data, then working to change laws and to affect public policy and programs. They tackled sanitation issues, truancy, infant mortality, drug use, minimum wages, labor rights, child-labor laws, and reliable, available public services.

"The Settlement [. . .] constantly acts between the various institutions of the city and the people for whose benefit these institutions were erected," wrote Jane. "Another function of the Settlement to its neighborhood resembles that of the big brother whose mere presence on the playground protects the little one from bullies."

WHAT THE WORLD

needs... is an outbreak of goodwill and human understanding.

THE HULL-HOUSE, CHICAGO

Hull-House had roughly ten thousand neighborhood people come through its buildings every week. The leading women social reformers of the times were all residents at certain points. Clearly, something was working. In fact, fifty years after a historic photo was taken in 1924 (*Meet the Hull-House Kids*), a newspaper tracked down several of the kids and found they grew up to become "lawyers and mechanics, sewer workers, dump truck drivers, [a] candy shop owner, a boxer, and [not so illustriously] a mob boss."

By moving into the poverty-stricken neighborhood and providing so many services *as neighbors,* Jane Addams and Hull-House were able to bridge a divide that the city had not been able to. And many of the neighbors were able to cross that bridge and finally get out—leaving poverty behind.

Jane Addams lived and worked at Hull-House until her death in 1935. She worked tirelessly for equality and peace—at the settlement, through her writings, and through many international efforts. In 1931, she was the corecipient of the Nobel Peace Prize. The settlement houses grew into a nationwide movement with more than five hundred houses in the United States—and with Hull-House the gold standard to be emulated.

DORIS TAYLOR
Supper for Seniors—Delivered

Mmmmm . . . dinner delivered straight to your door. Today there are apps for restaurants, for groceries, for pipin' hot pizza delivered lickety-split.

But long before delivery of fresh food was just a tap away, home-delivered meals were less a luxury indulgence and more a much-needed service. For many elderly people living on their own (and hoping to remain so), everyday meals weren't easy. And as the population of the elderly only continued to grow, caring for all of them became an increasing concern.

"No new plan for the aged had even been thought of," wrote *Doris Taylor, founder of Meals on Wheels, "and the need for it was growing greater and more urgent every day. The general idea of those trying to cope with it seemed to be that more Institutions— Old Folk's Homes—must be built for them."*

Instead, in 1953, Doris began Meals on Wheels in Australia— a distribution service of freshly cooked, nutritious meals delivered by volunteers to the homes of the elderly or homebound. Meals on Wheels organizations (all independently owned and operated) now exist throughout Australia, the United Kingdom, Ireland, Canada, and the United States—delivering hundreds of thousands of meals every year.

As a political and community worker, Doris (her own mobility dependent upon a wheelchair after a childhood accident left her paralyzed) saw the growing problem of food insecurity among the elderly. Many seniors simply did not have enough food, were not able to get out and about easily, or were not able to cook meals, and they weren't getting the proper nutrition to stay healthy. Just as importantly, due to her own health needs, Doris also intimately understood the importance of remaining independent as long as possible.

Meals on Wheels works as a nonprofit that relies on volunteers to deliver the meals and on recipients to pay for the cost of the meals (or receive a government subsidy that pays for them). Donations, grants, and fundraising efforts enable Meals on Wheels to run operations with a small paid staff, in addition to the thousands of volunteers it relies on.

"Meals on Wheels," wrote Doris, "is a scheme whereby one hot meal per day is taken to the home of aged and infirm people. It is a Social Service provided by the community. IT IS NOT A CHARITY—It is a Social experiment. An attempt to solve the problem of the care of the aged under modern conditions."

Doris borrowed the skeleton of the idea from similar programs she'd read about that had taken place during the Blitz (a bombing campaign against Britain during World War II), whereby women volunteers delivered meals to families whose homes had been destroyed by bombs.

She researched the need for such a program, speaking with social workers, doctors, police, and clergymen. She also read many reports. The consensus was that the need for such a program was strong—and growing stronger by the day. And though many people Doris contacted—the newspaper chief of staff, various politicians, potential benefactors—all expressed enthusiasm for the idea (and the *need* for such a program), there was also a consensus that it was utterly undoable.

And yet, Doris simply refused to take no for an answer from anyone whose help she required to get Meals on Wheels up and running. She traveled throughout South Australia in her motor-powered wheelchair, drumming up support.

Which she got.

With the Meals on Wheels model, seniors receive a hot, nutritious meal every day—and sometimes (depending on the specific local program) frozen meals as well. The delivery volunteers set up the hot meal on seniors' plates, visit and socialize with them for a few minutes, perform a brief safety check of the surroundings, and, when necessary, recommend community services that might be helpful to any individual's specific circumstances.

In America, one in four seniors lives alone and struggles with hunger, isolation, and usually financial strain as well. There are more than five thousand independent, locally operated Meals on Wheels programs throughout the United States. In 2019, the need for meals far exceeded the resources available, and many seniors wishing to participate were placed on long waitlists.

"The knowledge that organized help is available," wrote Doris, *"that [seniors] need never again depend on chance help or grudging help, or be left to suffer with no help at all, will bring comfort to the hearts and minds of every aged and infirm person."*

Today, roughly seventy years later, many seniors are able to stay in their own homes rather than go to nursing facilities precisely because of programs such as Meals on Wheels.

And it doesn't matter if Grandma isn't tech savvy enough to tap an app and have pipin' hot pizza delivered lickety-split— the doorbell will ring soon enough with her Meals on Wheels delivery . . . and it will be more nutritious!

KOMAL AHMAD
The World's Most Ridiculous Problem

"I'm starving!" she says. He says. They say.

For most of us, "I'm starving!" means it's been a few hours since lunch and, mmm, a little snack sounds good right about now.

For others, it means hours and hours—even days—have passed since their last meal, and a little snack sounds like a slice of heaven right about now.

"Every day in America," says Komal Ahmad, *"we waste over three hundred sixty-five million pounds of perfectly edible food. Meanwhile, in Silicon Valley—one of the wealthiest places in the*

world—one in four people don't know where their next meal will come from."

Komal founded the technology company Copia in 2012 to dramatically reduce food waste and solve the world's "dumbest" problem—hunger. Her company created a mobile app and web-based platform that connect those with excess food to those needing food—in real time—and then the company employees distribute it. By 2019, they had recovered more than two million pounds of food and distributed nearly three million meals.

"Clearly," Komal further explains, "it's not a lack of food that's the issue. It's an ineffective distribution of that food. So hunger [in the United States] is not a scarcity problem—it's a logistics problem."

Komal was moved to action when she was a student at the University of California, Berkeley. On her way to and from classes, she passed several homeless people, most of whom begged for money. One man, though, asked Komal for food, and something about that interaction compelled her to invite him to lunch. She learned he was a veteran still waiting for his benefits to kick in; he had no money and hadn't eaten in three days. Three. Whole. Days.

"And," Komal adds incredulously, "to add insult to injury, right across the street, Berkeley's dining hall was throwing away thousands of pounds of perfectly edible food . . . while those who needed it starved."

That was the moment she realized hunger in the United States was a "dumb" problem—and one she wanted to solve. She spoke to the dining hall manager about donating their excess food but was told it had to be thrown away. Komal suggested he could at least throw it away across the street in the park—so the homeless people there could eat it—but was told that, like donating, that posed a liability issue (the university could be sued if someone got sick). Later, though, Komal's research revealed that fear of legal action was no longer a problem due to recent legislation.

Persistence (and research!) paid off, and for the first iteration of her business Komal teamed up with the Berkeley dining hall and had students redistribute the hall's excess food to various shelters. She thought it was a good start, but the process was unpredictable. She'd be notified randomly if there was excess food; then she'd call shelter after shelter to see who wanted it. It was hugely inefficient. (She was once stuck with five hundred gourmet sandwiches after calling thirty nonprofits and not being able to find a place that needed them.)

The Bill Emerson Good Samaritan Act of 1996 was signed into law by President Bill Clinton to encourage food donations to nonprofits by minimizing liability issues.

"I remember thinking," says Komal, *"how much more effective and efficient it would be if those that had food could say, 'Hey, we have food,' and those that needed food could say, 'Hey, we could use that food.' We'd solve the problem for both of them. Essentially, we're match dot com for sandwiches!"*

So, she and her budding team created a technology solution connecting businesses, corporations, hospitals, restaurants, stadiums, and universities with excess food directly to nonprofit organizations in need of food—homeless shelters, afterschool programs, and veterans' agencies.

The process is simple. Using the app, a company inputs the kind of food they have, how much they have, and when and where it's available for pickup. Meanwhile, nonprofits enter their needs into the program (how many meals they need, any restrictions, etc.) as soon as those needs arise. An algorithm in the app takes the company with the excess food and matches it

In addition to not wasting food, the donating companies are able to claim a tax deduction. Copia also provides them with data and analytics that help them make better food purchasing decisions—very real and tangible benefits to the companies, who, in turn, pay Copia (a for-profit business) a fee to use the platform. And those fees fund the business.

REQUEST

RECOVER

REPORT

to the needs of a nonprofit within certain geographical perimeters, then dispatches drivers to pick up the food and deliver it.

"I have a fundamental annoyance with people who say 'no' or 'that's impossible,'" explains Komal, *"because I think it's just too easy—saying 'no' requires no action. 'Yes' requires action."*

And it's action that gets fresh food delivered to people who might not have eaten for days. And because of that, those people will no longer have to say, "I'm starving" . . . and actually mean it.

WANGARI MAATHAI
The Tree-Planting Plan

tep one: *dig a hole.*

Step two: plant a seedling in the hole.

Sometimes, the most complex problems respond to the simplest of solutions.

The list of complex problems plaguing many villages in Kenya was long: no fuel, no shelter, no clean water, no jobs. Malnourished people. Massive soil erosion. Increasing defor- estation . . .

Step three: water the seedling and nurture it.

As a biologist, native Kenyan Wangari Maathai understood

the interconnectedness between the environmental problems and the day-to-day living problems of the Kenyan people. Women would describe such problems to Wangari:

Every day, we walk farther and farther to get our firewood.

Our crops and livestock are not doing well—our food is scarce.

The streams providing our water are drying up.

Wangari understood that deforestation—chopping down large swaths of forest trees to make room for development—took away wood for fuel and shelter. It altered the environment, affecting waterways and soil composition (which affected crops and grazing livestock). She understood that the loss of deep tree roots caused soil erosion—leading to mudslides and polluted water.

"Now, it is one thing to understand the issues," wrote Wangari in her book, Unbowed. *"It is quite another to do something about them. But I have always been interested in finding solutions."*

Wangari devised a simple plan to address deforestation and many of the problems facing the Kenyan rural communities—plant trees. She instigated a tree-planting initiative in 1977 while serving on the National Council of Women of Kenya. It came to be known as the Green Belt Movement and, since its inception, has planted more than fifty-one million trees and counting!

"Tree planting became a natural choice to address some of the initial basic needs identified by women," said Wangari

Wangari Maathai was awarded the Nobel Peace Prize in 2004. The Nobel Committee stated that the award was "for her contribution to sustainable development, democracy and peace. Peace depends on our ability to secure our living environment. [. . .] She thinks globally and acts locally."

in her Nobel Lecture. *"Also, tree planting is simple, attainable and guarantees quick, successful results within a reasonable amount of time. This sustains interest and commitment."*

Wangari gave seedlings to rural Kenyan women to plant. She told them trees would begin to replenish the vanishing forests, and tree roots would grow deep and help keep the soil in place, slowing erosion. Trees would provide wood for cooking fuel and for fencing in livestock. And trees that bore fruit would provide food. She also paid the women a small wage, giving them a bit of money that allowed for a bit of independence. (Funding for the initiative came through extensive fundraising and donations.)

"Initially, the work was difficult," explains Wangari in her *Nobel Lecture, "because historically our people have been persuaded to believe that because they are poor, they lack not only capital, but also knowledge and skills to address their challenges [and therefore must rely on others, on government, to overcome their problems]."*

There certainly were challenges along the way. For example,

Wangari established a tree nursery to grow the seedlings and provide jobs to the women caring for them. But once, upon returning from a trip, she discovered all the seedlings had died due to lack of water because of a water shortage. The nursery collapsed and she was forced to start anew. Another challenge: Wangari tried to implement tree planting throughout all of Kenya, but none of those original efforts were sustained.

"I learned," Wangari wrote in Unbowed, *"that if you do not have local people who are committed to the process and willing to work with their communities, the projects will not survive."*

Still, with some time, and as more people got involved—such as farmers and groups from churches and schools—tree planting began to take off.

The key element was that these local communities were finally taking ownership of the planting and of the problems it addressed and solved. With that ownership, the people happily spread the mission of the Green Belt Movement to other communities, and those communities grew the movement to even more communities.

The Green Belt Movement has mobilized and trained more than thirty thousand Kenyan women to plant trees—positive proof that grassroots efforts can indeed effect change. The idea (and method) of tree planting has been adopted by other countries as well.

79

"As women and communities increased their efforts," Wangari wrote in Unbowed, *"we encouraged them to plant seedlings in rows of at least a thousand trees to form green 'belts' that would restore to the earth its cloth of green. This is how the name Green Belt Movement began to be used. Not only did the 'belts' hold the soil in place and provide shade and windbreaks but they also re-created habitat and enhanced the beauty of the landscape."*

Sometimes, the most complex problems respond to the simplest of solutions.

Step one: dig a hole.

Those trees *did* help solve some of the problems over time: The people had more access to shelter and fuel and food. Soil erosion slowed, and clean water returned to some areas.

Step two: plant . . . an idea.

Alongside the conservation efforts, the Green Belt Movement also began advocating for representative democracy in government.

Step three: . . . nurture it.

Kenyans held their first fully democratic election in a generation—and Wangari Maathai was elected to Parliament and was made a minister for the environment. To this day, holes are dug, seedlings are planted, watered, and nurtured . . . and the Kenyan environment continues its regrowth.

WHEN WE PLANT TREES, WE PLANT THE SEEDS OF PEACE, OF HOPE.

RADWA ROSTOM
Rebuilding Underprivileged Communities— The Eco-Friendly Way

ud. Sand. Gravel.

They can certainly make a mess—especially when tracked into a house.

But Radwa Rostom doesn't fret so much about those things inside a house—mainly because she thinks that mud, sand, and gravel should actually *be* the house.

Substandard housing exists in many parts of the world, including in Cairo, Egypt, where Radwa lives. There, more than sixteen *million* men, women, and children live in slums or substandard homes. They live in housing structures with walls made of tin sheets or cardboard, of cracked and crumbling bricks, blocks, and stones. There's no ventilation, no insulation, no sanitation.

"I've always had this idea that I wanted to do construction," says Radwa, *"and I wanted to do it in an environmentally friendly way, and I wanted to do it for the less-fortunate segment of the community."*

After graduating from college with a degree in engineering, Radwa started the Hand Over initiative in 2014 (incorporating it into a business in 2016). Her project had a lofty goal: rebuild houses and community buildings for the underprivileged using eco-friendly, sustainable materials—specifically, mud, sand, and gravel. By 2019, Radwa and Hand Over's construction projects had already helped more than *one thousand* people.

Her idea started simply. While she was an engineering student in Egypt, Radwa spent her free hours volunteering as a literacy tutor in a Cairo slum. On one such visit, she found herself completely distracted and dismayed by the disintegrating living conditions—large holes and cracks and crumbling walls. Instead of ignoring the problem, she decided to do something about it.

"One of the things I believe," Radwa explains, *"is that nothing is impossible. Even if the issue seems hopeless and requires a huge effort—you can at least take a small step and try to solve it."*

Her solution was to build environmentally friendly houses using a technique called rammed-earth construction. Equally important, she would train architectural and engineering students—along with local residents—in the technique and then connect the two groups to work together side by side.

"So the idea of earth construction," explains Radwa, "is that we mainly use earth materials: sand and mud and gravel, mixed in with water and a mixture that includes limestone. Sometimes we add a little cement, but never very much—a fraction compared to the conventional techniques of building."

Radwa chose the rammed-earth construction technique for several reasons:

1) It's very easy to teach.

2) It doesn't require heavy equipment.

3) It's very durable.

4) It provides good insulation for hot days.

5) The materials are sustainable, affordable, and available outside.

And importantly, by using earth building techniques, she's also tackling climate change—cutting more than 30% of carbon emissions that would normally come with projects made from nonsustainable materials such as concrete and steel (which have higher carbon footprints due to the necessity of extracting, manufacturing, and transporting).

Every day presents substantial challenges—including gaining the trust of the people she hopes to help. Even once construction began on her pilot project, the people remained skeptical.

"One day, it was raining," recalls Radwa, *"and they all thought, 'Oh, well, if it's raining, then the whole house will just fall down.' When they went to the house and saw that it was still standing, that it was still strong—that was the full realization and acceptance that this building was going to be fine."*

Radwa continues to evolve her business model. She's added another tract for private-sector projects—creating homes and buildings for people and companies who can afford to pay for the work—allowing her to generate profits, which, in turn, fund the core mission of rebuilding

In the beginning, Radwa had no idea how to start a business, make an action plan, do a study, or make money—any of those necessary skills to take her idea to the next level. Luckily, she was awarded a fellowship to the Do School in Germany. And there, she learned.

the underprivileged communities. Her hope is that the company will become self-sustaining and will also scale up.

"Someone needs to step ahead and say that we're solving it [a given problem]," says Radwa. *"I've always felt a responsibility for doing something for my community."*

And thanks to Radwa and Hand Over, the local community of Abu Ghaddan village (a very neglected rural area) now has its first school—filled with three hundred eager students.

Radwa was able to fund her pilot project with prize money she won from a social innovation contest. When that project succeeded, Radwa and Hand Over garnered a lot of publicity, which helped her land fellowships and grants, bringing in money for additional projects.

It's true that mud, sand, and gravel can make a big mess when tracked into a house. Radwa has also shown that mud, sand, and gravel can indeed *make* a house—as evidenced by her successful (and dry!) pilot project. She's also shown that she can make a world of difference rebuilding homes and public buildings for the underprivileged . . . helping not only millions of people but also the environment along the way.

LESLEY MARINCOLA
Making Solar Energy Affordable

Zap! An electric current zips through miles and miles of power lines to get to your house. Flip a switch—*ta-da!*—a light turns on. Plug in a cord, a cell phone charges.

But for those without electricity, those who live off-grid (and there are at least *one billion* such people around the world), the simple act of turning on a light is no small task.

It is a problem that Lesley Marincola and her company, Angaza, are trying to solve through a unique pay-as-you-go approach to solar-powered home energy systems.

"We make life-changing products—like solar lighting—afford-able and accessible to low-income, rural consumers in emerging markets," explains Lesley.

The struggles for those who live off-grid (in homes not hooked up to electricity) are real: having no light after dark, using lamps with dangerous kerosene (which can cause devastating fires and burns and is also toxic to breathe), walking miles to charge a battery, and losing crops due to lack of irrigation.

Though she had witnessed many people struggling without electricity through her travels, it wasn't until graduate school (where Lesley was pursuing product design and mechanical engineering) that she truly learned the global scale of energy poverty. It wasn't just difficult to access electrical power; even obtaining solar power was a challenge.

Angaza's distributors offer several pay-as-you-go solar products, such as lights, phone charging ports, batteries, radios, and water pumps. The technology can be customized for different languages, cultures, and financing options.

"The thing is," explains Lesley, *"solar products existed, but they weren't getting to the people who needed them most."*

She identified the primary barrier: up-front cost. A solar lamp might cost fifty to one hundred dollars. For a family earning only two dollars a day in places such as Nairobi and Uganda, saving enough money to make such a large purchase is essentially impossible.

"So," explains Lesley, *"we enable consumers to prepay from their cell phones in very small amounts—hourly, daily, weekly—for their energy."*

She drew from two existing business sectors for inspiration: microfinance (a form of banking in emerging markets that offers small "micro" loans) and the telecom industry (specifically prepaid cell phones). To fund Angaza in the early and growth stages, the for-profit company received financing from investment companies and venture capital firms in exchange for company stock (some ownership of Angaza).

It wasn't until her team did a small pilot project in rural Tanzania in 2012, working with families in approximately twenty homes, that Lesley first realized she and her team might really be on to something.

"We were using our own devices at that point," Lesley explains, *"and they were very much prototypes in every sense of the word—*

they were duct-taped together, hot-glued—literally just prototypes to show the concept."

Her small team lived in a Tanzanian village for several months, talking to the residents about their needs, testing out these pay-as-you-go solar-lighting prototypes. Once back in the United States, Lesley continued to receive micro payments from the Tanzanian people who kept these devices—and used them to light their homes—for almost a year!

"The fact that these twenty homes so valued these duct-taped, hot-glued prototypes—and how they were able to pay for them—was kind of the 'light bulb' that went off. And we were like, 'Okay, I think this is going to work at scale,'" says Lesley.

How it works:

- Mobile phones send and receive money using a mobile money application that is similar to text messaging (called USSD), with the mobile account tied to a phone's SIM card.
- Embedded technology is metered so the product turns on only for the amount of time paid for.
- A small down payment (~5%) allows people to take the solar product home.
- The micro-usage payments add up toward the outright purchase of the product (generally in six to twelve months).
- The consumer then has unlimited, free solar power.

Early on, Angaza created their own solar lights and embedded their pay-as-you-go technology inside. It quickly became obvious, though, that making their own products was unnecessary because plenty of manufacturers were already making good-quality solar products. So instead, the company partnered with manufacturers who embedded Angaza's technology into the solar products already being made.

Lesley's goal is to reach one hundred million people living off-grid in the next five years. She and the team at Angaza are well on their way: they work with solar distribution companies in more than fifty countries—including Kenya, Bangladesh, and Nicaragua—and support millions of loans on their technology platform . . . and those numbers continue to rise.

Living off-grid means there's no zap of electricity to power things up. But now, using sunbeams, solar panels, and cell phones (and some ingenious technology behind the scenes), it takes one push of a button and . . . *ta-da!* A light turns on in a one-room home, allowing the kids to complete their home-work. An irrigation system turns on to water thirsty crops, making it likely they'll survive until harvest.

Life-changing indeed.

TARA CHKLOVSKI

Inspiring Girls to Succeed in Tech

Something unusual was going on. Girls—thousands of them, scattered around the globe—were practically glued to their cell phones all day. And all night. For three months. But . . . they weren't texting. Or Snapchatting. Or posting Instagram stories.

Instead, they were designing apps and writing code. They were taking part in the Technovation Challenge—spearheaded by Tara Chklovski and her nonprofit parent company, Iridescent.

"I started Iridescent [in 2006] to inspire girls and women and

underserved communities," explains Tara, "and to have them experience very powerful, real-world examples of how engineering and technology can make a difference."

Initially she did this through afterschool programs—with engineering students teaching younger girls topics such as the physics of sailing and amusement parks.

By inspiring girls in particular, Tara hoped to address a very troubling problem head-on—the dramatic absence of women in technology fields. Tech is one of the largest growing employment sectors, and yet 80% of those jobs are filled by men—meaning opportunities for innovation and career advancement are lost for women.

The Technovation Challenge—a technology-based competition started in 2010 for girls ages ten to eighteen—is Tara's flagship program. The idea centers on designing a working app that solves a real-world problem in their community—such as food insecurity

The competition begins online and is a twelve-week process. Technovation provides the technology platform, the connections to mentors, local resources, and a step-by-step curriculum that guides the girls along the way. Technovation is a nonprofit that gets funding from grants, donations, fundraising, and sponsorships from tech companies such as Google, Adobe, Uber, and Salesforce.

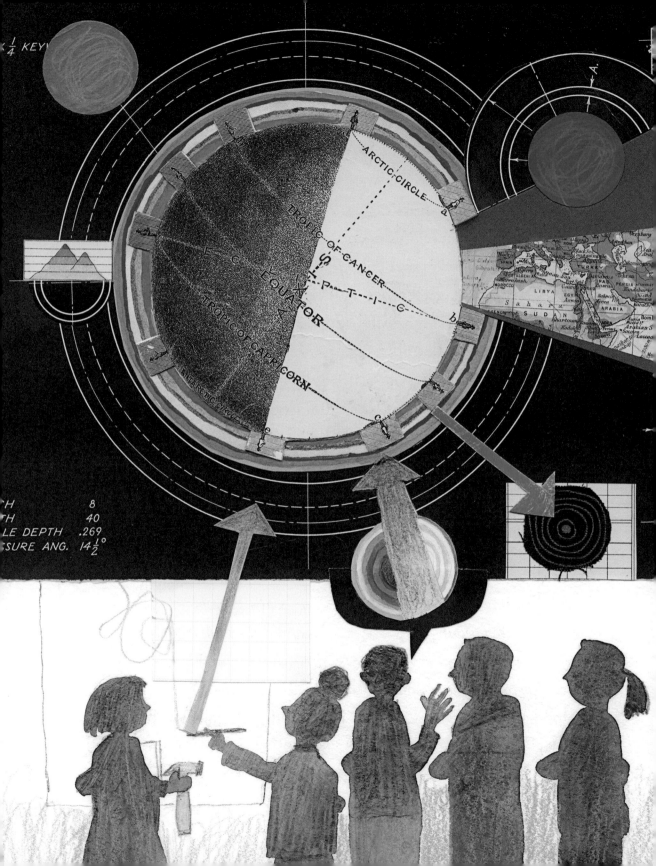

or street safety. In 2018, twenty thousand girls participated from all over the world!

Using a mobile phone to create an app was a logical entry point for engaging girls with technology.

"I think it's very clear," explains Tara, *"that women and girls—especially teenagers—are big users of cell phones. But girls don't usually see themselves as creators of this technology. They don't open an app and say, 'Oh, I can make a better one.'"*

Building Technovation came with a number of challenges—beginning with the competition task itself. In the first two years, teams were allowed to create an app about anything that excited them. Tara was dismayed when nearly all entrants went with the stereotypical female topic of fashion. By year three, Tara and her team prescribed specific categories from which the girls had to choose (and fashion was not one of them).

"And all the girls rebelled," recalls Tara. *"They said, 'We don't have any ideas around STEM education or health care . . .' But then, when they actually sat down to think about it, the girls came up with such interesting ideas. We got all sorts of innovative games; we got a cool app around helping teens with diabetes [and one on first aid, and another on how to dissect a frog!] And the girls were just stunned by what they could come up with when they were challenged."*

In year four, the task of the Technovation Challenge had evolved to its current status: develop an app that would in some way help the community. This was broad enough to engage the girls and let them choose something that interested them . . . while also challenging them to create something that was impactful.

One team from Nigeria invented an app that identified fake prescription drugs, which put patients' lives in danger.

A team from India created an app that connected e-waste producers (old computers are e-waste, for example) directly with authorized recyclers, so as not to harm the environment.

And a team from the United States built an app that works like a virtual speech therapist, helping kids with speech pronunciation.

Five girls from Kazakhstan won in 2017 with their app QamCare, a personal security system (especially for walking alone after dark). The app allows users to tap an SOS button that instantly sends their location to family and other contacts listed. The team even created a panic button— paired to the app with Bluetooth—that can be in a pocket or worn around the neck.

"It's a whole other thing, of course, to take an idea to market and build it up," says Tara, "but I think the message is you need to be looking for innovation in different places and to tell girls they're capable of

it—and then you give them the skills by which they can make that idea a reality."

Through Technovation, Tara exposes girls to technology, gives them hands-on tech experience, and lets them know she believes in their ability to succeed. She describes Technovation as a very safe sandbox in which the girls can try something that might be a bit hard but gives them a great sense of accomplishment.

"That sense of empowerment is absolutely life-changing," says Tara.

Give a girl a cell phone—and an opportunity to learn the technology within it—and she just might be up late at night texting or Snapchatting with friends about a great idea for an app that just might solve online bullying, or school lunch waste, or overpackaging, or maybe . . .

YOUR TURN
Saving the World One Solution at a Time

In the San Fernando Valley of California, thousands and thousands of homeless people have no choice but to sleep outside. So, when Maggie Mejia and America Hernandez—along with ten other girls at their high school—joined DIY Girls, a STEM-based program that tasked them to help solve a problem in their community, they all agreed to tackle homelessness.

"We come from a low-income community," explains America, *"and many of our families live paycheck by paycheck. We all under-*

stood what it might be like—if someone doesn't bring home a pay-check—how we might be homeless ourselves."

So they invented an amazing portable tent that rolls into a backpack, has solar power, and also contains a sanitary cleansing mechanism. Every element in the process was new to them: coding, using power tools, fixing machines that broke—and yet, they did it! As of 2019, the tent remained a prototype and had not yet been mass-produced or distributed—though that doesn't mean it won't ever be.

It is a promising start, and a new question arises: What other problems might girls apply their skills to—to brainstorm, research, innovate . . . and potentially solve?

In fact, what problems might *you* tackle—to brainstorm, to research, to innovate, to potentially solve? Are you ready to change the world?

A good place to start might be with two of the profiles you just read about:

1. Technovation: technovation.org
2. RandomKid: randomkid.org

If you've already been developing an idea, perhaps you're ready to try out a competition? There are a number of social entrepreneur contests and competitions that award prize money, mentors, resources, and help to get your venture off the ground. Here are just a few:

1. Ashoka Youth Venture: youthventure.org
2. World Series of Innovation (ages 13–24): innovation.nfte.com
3. Youth Citizen Entrepreneurship Competition (ages 15–35), through the United Nations: un.org
4. Staples Youth Social Entrepreneur Competition (ages 12–24): changemakers.com
5. The Paradigm Challenge (students ages 4–18): projectparadigm.org

What great need do you see in the world that requires action? How might you go about changing it? Remember, having a great idea for a social enterprise is just step one. Steps two through . . . ten? . . . fifty? . . . a hundred? will undoubtedly bring struggles and hardships in the effort to make your idea a reality. It's often difficult to fundraise—trying to convince investors or donators to give you money for your venture. It's exhausting in the early days—working many hours, giving up free time just to get your vision off the ground.

But persistence pays off. Believing in yourself and your idea and "never taking no for an answer" pay off.

Look around. Everywhere, there are problems—big and small. But also everywhere, there is hope.

The world currently awaits your innovative idea . . .

You've got this!

Glossary of Business Terms

Action plan: a proposed strategy

Affiliate: a person or company that is officially attached or connected to an organization

Algorithm: a process or set of rules followed in calculations, especially by a computer, in order to solve a problem

Automation: automatically controlled operation of a device or process; doing the work of human labor

Business model: a design for the successful operation of a business

Business plan: a proposal detailing a business's objectives and means to achieve them

Capital: money or other valuable financial assets

Consulting: giving expert advice to people working in a given profession

Consumer: a person who purchases goods and services

Crowdfunding: raising small amounts of money from a large number of people, usually on the internet

Entrepreneur: a person who starts a business and assumes the risks involved with starting such a business (financial, legal, working hours, personnel, etc.)

Fellowship: a highly selective position, for a specified period of time, and generally for training or study, that comes with payment

Financing: providing funding (of money) for a person or organization

For-profit: a company with a goal to make money, make a profit

Funding: money provided for a particular purpose

Fundraising: trying to generate financial support (i.e., receive money) for an organization

Grant: money given by the government or an organization for a specific purpose (grant money is given to the recipient; it is not a loan)

Infrastructure: the underlying foundation and resources of a business (buildings, equipment, personnel, systems, etc.)

Investor: a person or organization that puts money into a company (or other venture) with the expectation that the investor will earn a profit

Iteration: the act or process of repeating, trying to successively get closer to the desired result

Microfinance: financial services for impoverished individuals or groups; usually given in the form of microloans (very small amounts of money given upfront to be repaid little by little over time)

Nonprofit: a business that is not conducted with the goal of financially profiting but rather to further charitable objectives

Outsourcing: obtaining goods or services from outside a company (often from a foreign source)

Parent company: a corporation that owns controlling interest in another company

Platform: (specifically, digital platform) the place (or environment) where software (such as an app, a browser, or an operating system) is executed

Product development: the process of bringing a product through all stages from design to market

Prototype/prototyping: a preliminary model of something to test the design; testing a design with a preliminary model

Scale up: to increase in size or number; to expand

Seed funding: initial funding (of money) used to start a business

Sponsorship: financial support given from a sponsor

Stock: (also **share** or **equity**) a type of security that indicates partial, proportionate ownership of a company

Vendor: a person or company offering something for sale

Venture capital: capital (money) invested in a company or project (usually new) where there is substantial risk

Wall Street: a street in New York City where the stock exchange and financial businesses are located

Quoted Sources

Addams, Jane. *Twenty Years at Hull-House (with Autobiographical Notes)*. New York: MacMillan, 1912.

Ahmad, Komal, interview by the author, June 2018.

Billimoria, Jeroo, interview by the author, June 2018.

Chen, Jane, interview by the author, July 2018.

Chklovski, Tara, interview by the author, June 2018.

Doromal, Lisa, interview by the author, July 2018.

The First Annual Report of the Managers of the Ladies' Depository; With a List of the Officers and Managers, and of the Contributors. Philadelphia: Printed by Order of the Society, Lydia R. Bailey, 1834.

Garrard, Alice. "Wendy Kopp, CEO/Founder, Teach for America: Reaping the Rewards of High Expectations." Philanthropy News Digest, January 30, 2009. philanthropynewsdigest.org/newsmakers/wendy-kopp-ceo-founder-teach-for-america-reaping-the-rewards-of-high-expectations.

Gaudiani, Claire, and David Graham Burnett. *Daughters of the Declaration: How Women Social Entrepreneurs Built the American Dream*. New York: PublicAffairs, 2011.

Hamilton, Nadia, interview by the author, July 2018.

Hernandez, America, interview by the author, June 2018.

Kopp, Wendy, interview by Guy Raz. "Teach for America: Wendy Kopp."
   How I Built This with Guy Raz, NPR, October 9, 2017.
   npr.org/2019/07/05/738989797/teach-for-america-wendy-kopp.

Kopp, Wendy. *One Day, All Children . . .* New York: PublicAffairs, 2001.

Leman, Talia, interview by the author, June 2018.

Lowe, Brendan (former director of communications, Teach For All), interview
   by the author, June 2018.

Lublin, Nancy, interview by Jessica Harris. "Nancy Lublin, Founder of Dress
   for Success." *From Scratch,* NPR, May 25, 2011. npr.org/2011/05/25/
   136649621/nancy-lublin-founder-of-dress-for-success.

Lublin, Nancy, interview by the author, July 2018.

Maathai, Wangari. "Nobel Lecture." Lecture presented at the 2004 Nobel
   Peace Prize Presentation, Oslo, Norway, December 10, 2004. nobelprize
   .org/prizes/peace/2004/maathai/26050-wangari-maathai-nobel-
   lecture-2004.

Maathai, Wangari. *Unbowed.* New York: First Anchor Books, 2006.

Marincola, Lesley, interview by the author, July 2018.

Mejia, Maggie, interview by the author, June 2018.

Rostom, Radwa, interview by the author, June 2018.

Shih, Ting, interview by the author, June 2018.

Taylor, Doris. *Meals on Wheels: What It Is – How It Began – What It Is Now – What It Can Become!* (16-page pamphlet). Adelaide, South Australia: Griffin Press, 1964.

Wadler, Joyce. "Looking Sharp, Landing Jobs; Gifts of Clothing Help Poor Women to Find Work." *New York Times,* December 28, 1997. nytimes .com/1997/12/28/nyregion/looking-sharp-landing-jobs-gifts-of-clothing-help-poor-women-to-find-work.html.

Quoted Sources Within Illustrations

Page 13: Pastorek, Whitney. "Kids Want to Make a Difference, Too—RandomKid Lets Them Do It Themselves." *Fast Company,* December 9, 2013. www.fastcompany.com/3020786/kids-want-to-make-a-difference-too-randomkid-lets-them-do-it-themselves.

Page 19: Bornstein, David. *How to Change the World: Social Entrepreneurs and the Power of New Ideas.* New York: Oxford University Press, 2007.

Page 25: Garrard, Alice. "Wendy Kopp, CEO/Founder, Teach for America: Reaping the Rewards of High Expectations." Philanthropy News Digest, January 30, 2009. philanthropynewsdigest.org/newsmakers/wendy-kopp-ceo-founder-teach-for-america-reaping-the-rewards-of-high-expectations.

Page 48: Forleo, Marie. "How Nancy Lublin Turned Texting into a Life-Saving Nonprofit." Marie Forleo (blog). June 26, 2018. www.marieforleo .com/2018/06/nancy-lublin-interview.

Page 54: Waters Sander, Kathleen. *The Business of Charity: The Woman's Exchange Movement, 1832–1900.* Chicago: University of Illinois Press, 1998.

Page 62: Addams, Jane. *Jane Addams's Essays and Speeches on Peace.* Edited by Marilyn Fischer and Judy D. Whipps. New York: Continuum, New Edition, 2016. See esp. p. 337, "How to Build a Peace Program."

Page 72: Ahmad, Komal. "Keynote Address." Keynote address presented at the United Nations headquarters, New York City, June 6, 2016.

Page 81: The Green Belt Movement. "Homepage." greenbeltmovement.org. Accessed July 1, 2020.

Additional Sources

Ashoka: Everyone a Changemaker: ashoka.org/en-US

Bornstein, David. *How to Change the World: Social Entrepreneurs and the Power of New Ideas.* New York: Oxford University Press, 2007.

Bornstein, David, and Susan Davis. *Social Entrepreneurship: What Everyone Needs to Know.* New York: Oxford University Press, 2010.

Bosma, Niels, Stephen Hill, Aileen Ionescu-Somers, Donna Kelley, Jonathan Levie, and Anna Tarnawa. *Global Entrepreneurship Monitor 2019/2020 Global Report.* London: Global Entrepreneurship Research Association, London Business School, 2020. gemconsortium.org/report.

Centre for Social Innovation: socialinnovation.org

Echoing Green: echoinggreen.org

Elkington, John, and Pamela Hartigan. *The Power of Unreasonable People: How Social Entrepreneurs Create Markets That Change the World.* Boston: Harvard Business Press, 2008.

Encyclopedia.com. "Married Women's Property Act of 1848." encyclopedia.com/social-sciences/applied-and-social-sciences-magazines/married-womens-property-act-1848. Accessed May 31, 2020.

Forbes. "30 Under 30 Social Entrepreneurs." forbes.com/30-under-30/2018/social-entrepreneurs/#4a1a7a9e29e5. Accessed July 1, 2020.

girltank: girltank.org

Harvard Business Review. "Disruptive Innovation for Social Change." hbr.org/2006/12/disruptive-innovation-for-social-change. Accessed July 1, 2020.

Hewitt, Nancy A. *Women's Activism and Social Change: Rochester, New York, 1822–1872.* Ithaca, NY: Cornell University Press, 1984.

Intel International Science and Engineering Fair: newsroom.intel.com/press-kits/2019-isef

Leman, Talia. *A Random Book About the Power of Anyone.* New York: Free Press, 2012.

Lesonsky, Rieva. "The State of Women Entrepreneurs." SCORE, March 24, 2020. score.org/blog/state-women-entrepreneurs.

Lionesses of Africa: The Pride of Africa's Women Entrepreneurs. "Meet 38 Women Social Entrepreneurs Who Made a Major Impact in Africa in 2015." January 11, 2016. lionessesofafrica.com/blog/2016/1/10/meet-38-women-social-entrepreneurs-who-made-a-major-impact-in-africa-in-2015.

Maathai, Wangari. *The Green Belt Movement.* New York: Lantern Books, 2006.

McGee, Suzanne, and Heidi Moore. "Women's Rights and Their Money: A Timeline from Cleopatra to Lilly Ledbetter." *Guardian,* August 11, 2014. theguardian.com/money/us-money-blog/2014/aug/11/women-rights-money-timeline-history.

Milligan, Susan. "Stepping Through History: A Timeline of Women's Rights from 1769 to the 2017 Women's March on Washington." *U.S. News &*

World Report, January 20, 2017. usnews.com/news/the-report/
articles/2017-01-20/timeline-the-womens-rights-movement-in-the-us.

National Archives. "Women's Rights Timeline." archives.gov/women/timeline.
Accessed July 1, 2020.

National Women's History Alliance. "Detailed Timeline: Timeline of Legal
History of Women in the United States." nationalwomenshistoryalliance
.org/resources/womens-rights-movement/detailed-timeline.
Accessed July 1, 2020.

Ogunte: ogunte.com/innovation

Pinker, Steven. "Is the World Getting Better or Worse? A Look at the Numbers." TED Talk presented at an official TED conference, April 2018. ted
.com/talks/steven_pinker_is_the_world_getting_better_or_worse_a_look_
at_the_numbers?nolanguage=enBella.

SBDCNet. "Women in Business: A Brief History." March 26, 2019. sbdcnet
.org/sbdc-national-blog/women-in-business-brief-history.

Schwab Foundation for Social Entrepreneurship: schwabfound.org

Skoll Foundation: skoll.org

Stanford Social Innovation Review: ssir.org

Thimmesh, Catherine. *Girls Think of Everything.* Boston: Houghton Mifflin
Harcourt, 2000.

Toyota. "2017 Mothers of Invention: Remarkable Women, Changing the

World." Paid post in the *New York Times*. www.nytimes.com/paidpost/
toyota/mothers-of-invention-presented-by-women-in-the-world.html.
Accessed July 1, 2020.

U.S. News & World Report. "Historic Firsts in Women's Education in the
United States." Education, March 11, 2009. usnews.com/education/
articles/2009/03/11/historic-firsts-in-womens-education-in-the-united-
states.

Waters Sander, Kathleen. *The Business of Charity: The Woman's Exchange
Movement, 1832–1900*. Chicago: University of Illinois Press, 1998.

Featured Websites

Angaza: angaza.com

Childline India: childlineindia.org

ClickMedix: clickmedix.com

Copia: gocopia.com

DIY Girls: diygirls.org/sfhsinventeams

Dress for Success: dressforsuccess.org

Embrace Innovations: embraceinnovations.com

The Green Belt Movement: greenbeltmovement.org

Hand Over: ashoka.org/en-us/fellow/radwa-rostom

The History Channel: history.com

Magnusmode: magnusmode.com

Meals on Wheels: mealsonwheels.org.au; mealsonwheelsamerica.org

Our World in Data: ourworldindata.org

Pew Research Center: pewresearch.org

RandomKid: randomkid.org

Teach For America: teachforamerica.org

Technovation: technovation.org

United Nations: un.org

UN Women: unwomen.org

Acknowledgments

The author wishes to thank the following for their contributions:

Komal Ahmad, Jeroo Billimoria, Jane Chen, Tara Chklovski, Lisa Doromal, Nadia Hamilton, America Hernandez, Wendy Kopp, Brendan Lowe, Talia Leman, Dana Leman, Nancy Lublin, Lesley Marincola, Maggie Mejia, Radwa Rostom, Ting Shih, Meals on Wheels, Ashoka, Echoing Green, Ogunte, Schwab Foundation, Skoll Foundation, *Global Entrepreneurship Monitor*; my fabulous editor, Ann Rider; and the extraordinarily talented team at Houghton Mifflin Harcourt. Lastly, a special thanks to RFT, who passed away in April 2021, for all his love and support.

Index

About the Author and Illustrator

CATHERINE THIMMESH is the award-winning author of many books for children, including *Team Moon,* winner of the Sibert Medal; *Camp Panda,* a Sibert Honor winner; and *Friends: True Stories of Extraordinary Animal Friendships.* When researching projects, she uses primary sources—especially personal interviews—whenever possible. She believes the intimacy, emotion, and unexpected details that emerge from them strengthen her storytelling. As a child, Catherine had lots of business ideas, though she never implemented them. Along with other kids in her neighborhood, she loved creating homemade carnivals from preordered kits that raised money for charities. You can visit her online at catherinethimmesh.com.

MELISSA SWEET is the Caldecott Honor–winning illustrator of many children's books including *Some Writer! The Story of E. B. White,* winner of the NCTE Orbis Pictus Award; *Balloons Over Broadway,* a Sibert Medal winner; and *The Right Word* and *A River of Words,* both Caldecott Honor winners. Reviewers have described her unique mixed-media illustrations as "exuberant," "outstanding," and "a creative delight." As a child, Melissa started her own doughnut delivery business, and when she was told girls couldn't take mechanical or woodshop classes, she figured out a way to be the first girl in school to take them. She writes, "Figuring things out was the most exciting thing in the world to me, and learning how to use tools and materials was an important part of my education." Visit her online at melissasweet.net.

Don't Miss:

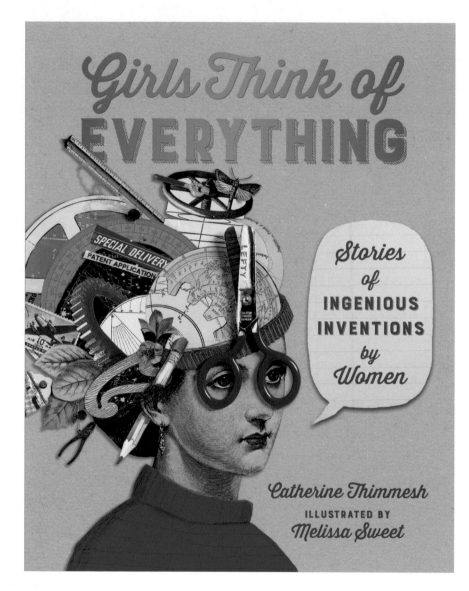

"As informative as it is empowering."
—*Horn Book*

"An outstanding collective biography of women and girls
who changed the world with their inventions."
—*School Library Journal*

QUIZ (CONTINUED)

True or False

1 American women entered the labor force in large numbers in the 1940s, because thousands of essential jobs needed to be filled when men went to fight in World War II.

2 In 2016, women in the United States made up 46.8% of the American workforce. At that time, the United States had the highest percentage of women in the workforce out of 114 countries surveyed.

3 Globally, women are paid between seventy and ninety cents for every one dollar a man is paid (even for the same job).

4 Prior to 1974, a woman could be denied credit (a credit card, mortgage, bank loan, etc.) in her own name simply because she was a woman (unless she brought a man along to cosign).

Answers:

1. True [For the first time, women were hired as taxi drivers, construction workers, and steel workers, for example.]

2. False [Thirty-nine countries ranked higher than the United States, with Zimbabwe on top with 52.8% of its workforce female.]

3. True [This is known as the gender pay gap. In the United States, the Equal Pay Act—which provides equal pay for equal work—was passed in 1963. Even so, in 2020, the gap was eighty-one cents paid to women for every one dollar paid to men.]

4. True [The Equal Credit Opportunity Act of 1974 changed this.]

Multiple Choice

1 In the United States, women make up 46% of the total workforce (as of 2019). What percentage of women (in the United States) make up the workforce for social enterprises (businesses that strive to benefit society and the environment)?

    a. 46%

    b. 25%

    c. 65%

    d. 80%

2 What percentage of women who have started social enterprises (out of five countries surveyed, including the United States) report an increase in their sense of self-worth?

    a. 75%

    b. 60%

    c. 42%

    d. 35%

3 In the United States in 2017, $85 billion in venture capital backing (investors giving money to a company) was invested in new entrepreneurial start-ups (both for-profit and nonprofit). How much of that money was invested with female entrepreneurs?

    a. 55%

    b. 49%

    c. 26%

    d. 2%